The Power of Penny Pinching

How to Reduce Debt on a Tight Budget

Benjamin Warson

Copyright © 2023 Benjamin Warson
All rights reserved.

Table of contents

Introduction 3

Chapter 1: The importance of reducing debt 6

Chapter 2: Budgeting 15

Chapter 3: Saving Strategies 27

Chapter 4: Debt Reduction Techniques 38

Chapter 5: Debt Relief Programs for Low-Income Families 50

Chapter 6: The Psychology of Money 60

Chapter 7: Long-Term Financial Planning 70

Chapter 8: Conclusion 79

About the author 87

Introduction

Debt can be a burden on anyone, but it can be especially challenging for those living on a tight budget. However, there are ways to reduce debt and achieve financial freedom, even if you are living paycheck to paycheck. In this chapter, we will explore the power of penny pinching and how it can help you reduce debt on a tight budget.

Budgeting and Saving

The first step in reducing debt is to create a budget. This will help you track your income and expenses and identify areas where you can cut back. Start by listing all your sources of income and your monthly expenses, including rent/mortgage, utilities, food, transportation, and any debt payments. Once you have a clear picture of your finances, you can start to identify areas where you can save money.

One easy way to save money is to reduce your food expenses. Plan your meals in advance and shop for groceries with a list. Avoid eating out and instead, cook at home. You can also look for coupons and deals to save money on groceries. Another way to save money is to reduce your energy bills. Turn off lights and electronics when you are not using them and unplug appliances that are not in use.
You can also adjust your thermostat to save on heating and cooling costs.

Debt Relief for Low-Income Families
If you are struggling with debt, there are options available to help you. One option is debt consolidation, which involves combining multiple debts into one loan with a lower interest rate. This can make it easier to manage your payments and reduce the amount of interest you pay over time.

Another option is debt settlement, which involves negotiating with creditors to settle your debt for less than what you owe.

This can be a good option if you are unable to make your payments and are facing debt collection actions. Reducing debt on a tight budget may seem impossible, but with the power of penny pinching, it can be done.

By creating a budget, saving money, and exploring debt relief options, you can take control of your finances and achieve financial freedom.

Remember, every penny counts, so start saving today!

Chapter 1: The importance of reducing debt

The importance of reducing debt cannot be overstated, especially for low-income families struggling to make ends meet.

Debt can cause financial stress, impact credit scores, and limit future opportunities.

However, reducing debt is not impossible, and there are several ways to achieve this goal.

One of the most effective ways to reduce debt is through budgeting and saving.

This involves creating a realistic budget that considers all monthly expenses, including bills, groceries, and entertainment.

By tracking expenses and cutting back on unnecessary spending, families can free up more money to pay off debt.

Another way to reduce debt is by seeking debt relief options. Many low-income families may qualify for debt relief programs, such as debt consolidation, debt settlement, or even bankruptcy. These programs can help lower monthly payments and reduce overall debt, making it more manageable for families to pay off.

Reducing debt is also crucial for parents who want to provide a better future for their children. High levels of debt can limit opportunities for parents to provide their children with a quality education, safe housing, and other necessities. By reducing debt, parents can free up more money to invest in their children's future and create a more stable financial situation for their family.

Reducing debt takes time and effort, but it is possible. By creating a budget, seeking debt relief options, and making smart financial decisions, families can reduce their debt and build a brighter financial future. It is important to remember that reducing debt is a journey, and it may take time to achieve the desired outcome. However, by staying committed and focused on the end goal, families can achieve financial freedom and provide a better life for their loved ones.

Understanding the impact of debt on low-income families

For low-income families, debt can be a vicious cycle that is difficult to break. It can lead to stress, anxiety, and a sense of hopelessness. Understanding the impact of debt on low-income families is crucial to finding ways to break this cycle and move towards financial stability.

One of the biggest impacts of debt on low-income families is the strain it places on their already limited resources.

When a family is already struggling to make ends meet, adding debt payments to the mix can be overwhelming. This can lead to difficult choices such as deciding between paying for food or paying off debt.

Debt can also have a negative impact on a family's credit score, making it harder to access credit in the future. This can lead to higher interest rates on loans, credit cards, and other financial products, making it even harder to get out of debt.

Another impact of debt on low-income families is the mental and emotional toll it takes. Constant worry about debt can lead to stress, anxiety, and depression.

This can affect not only the individual with the debt but also their family members.

To break the cycle of debt, it is important to start with a budget. Creating a budget can help low-income families understand where their money is going and identify areas where they can cut back. This can free up money to put towards debt payments.

Saving is also key to reducing debt.

Even small amounts saved each month can add up over time and help pay off debt faster. This may mean making sacrifices such as cutting back on entertainment or eating out, but it can be worth it in the long run.

Debt relief programs can also be helpful for low-income families struggling with debt.

These programs can offer assistance with negotiating with creditors, consolidating debt, and reducing interest rates. It is important to do research and find a reputable debt relief program to avoid scams.

Debt can have a significant impact on low-income families, but there are steps that can be taken to break the cycle.

The benefits of penny pinching

The benefits of penny pinching are numerous and can have a significant impact on your financial situation. For those struggling with debt reduction through budgeting and saving, penny pinching can be a powerful tool to help reduce debt and save money.

Here are some of the benefits of penny pinching that you can enjoy:

1. Helps you save more money: When you penny pinch, you're able to save more money. This is because you're cutting back on unnecessary expenses, which frees up more money that you can use to pay off debt or save for a rainy day.

2. Helps you pay off debt faster: One of the primary goals of penny pinching is to reduce debt. By cutting back on expenses and redirecting more money towards debt payments, you can pay off your debt faster and become debt-free sooner.

3. Helps you build better financial habits: Penny pinching requires discipline, patience, and planning. By developing these skills, you can build better financial habits that will help you manage your money more effectively in the long run.

4. Helps you avoid financial stress: Financial stress is a common problem for many people, especially those with low incomes. By penny pinching, you can reduce your financial stress by having more control over your money and knowing that you have a plan in place to manage your finances.

5. Helps you achieve your financial goals: Whether you want to save for a down payment on a home, pay off debt, or build an emergency fund, penny pinching can help you achieve your financial goals. By saving more money and reducing debt, you can put yourself in a better financial position to achieve your dreams.

For low-income families, penny pinching can be a lifeline for debt relief. By cutting back on expenses and saving more money, you can reduce your debt and build a better financial future for yourself and your family.

With dedication and perseverance, anyone can benefit from the power of penny pinching.

Chapter 2: Budgeting

The first step towards reducing debt on a tight budget is setting achievable financial goals. These goals will not only help you stay on track, but they will also provide you with a sense of accomplishment as you achieve each one. Start by identifying your priorities.

What do you want to achieve financially?

Do you want to pay off your high-interest credit card debt?

Or, do you want to save for a down payment on a new home?

Whatever your priorities may be, it is important to write them down and create a plan to achieve them.

When setting financial goals, it is important to make them measurable and specific.

For example, instead of saying, "I want to save money," say, "I want to save $500 in the next three months." This way, you will have a clear idea of what you are working towards and can track your progress along the way.

Another important factor to consider when setting financial goals is to make them realistic. If you set goals that are too lofty, you may become discouraged when you do not achieve them. Instead, start small and gradually increase your goals as you become more financially stable. Once you have identified your financial goals, it is important to create a budget to help you achieve them. A budget will allow you to see where your money is going and help you identify areas where you can cut back on expenses. By creating a realistic budget and sticking to it, you can reduce debt and achieve your financial goals.

Setting achievable financial goals is the first step towards reducing debt on a tight budget. By identifying your priorities, making them measurable and specific, and creating a realistic budget, you can stay on track and achieve financial stability. With dedication and persistence, you can take control of your finances and create a brighter financial future for yourself and your family.Creating a budget plan

Creating a Budget Plan

Budgeting is one of the most important steps to reducing debt on a tight budget. It is a financial plan that helps you manage your income and expenses. A budget plan helps you to determine how much money you have coming in, how much you are spending, and how to allocate your income to meet your needs and save for the future.

Here are some tips to help you create a budget plan that works for you:

Step 1: Calculate your incomeThe first step in creating a budget plan is to calculate your income. This includes your salary, wages, tips, and any other sources of income. It is important to be honest and accurate about your income because it will help you to determine how much money you have available to spend.

Step 2: List your expenses The next step is to list all of your expenses. This includes your rent or mortgage, utilities, phone bill, groceries, transportation, entertainment, and any other expenses you have. It is important to be thorough when listing your expenses so that you don't forget anything.

Step 3: Categorize your expenses After listing your expenses, it's important to categorize them. You can categorize them into fixed expenses (rent, utilities, etc.), variable expenses (groceries, entertainment, etc.), and discretionary expenses (eating out, shopping, etc.). This will help you to determine which expenses you can reduce or eliminate to save money.

Step 4: Set financial goalsSetting financial goals is an important part of creating a budget plan. Your financial goals may include paying off debt, saving for emergencies, or investing for the future. Your budget plan should reflect your financial goals and help you to achieve them.

Step 5: Allocate your incomeAfter calculating your income, listing your expenses, categorizing them, and setting financial goals, it's time to allocate your income. This means dividing your income into categories such as fixed expenses, variable expenses, and discretionary expenses. You should also allocate some of your income towards your financial goals.

By following these steps, you can create a budget plan that works for you.

Remember to be honest and accurate about your income and expenses, categorize your expenses, set financial goals, and allocate your income. With a budget plan in place, you can reduce debt on a tight budget and achieve financial freedom.

Tracking expenses
Tracking expenses is an essential step towards reducing debt and achieving financial stability. It is especially crucial for low-income families who are struggling to make ends meet.
By tracking expenses, you can identify where your money is going and where you can cut back on unnecessary spending.
One of the easiest ways to track your expenses is to use a budgeting app or software.

These tools allow you to input your income and expenses, and they will automatically categorize your spending. You can also set up alerts to notify you when you are approaching your budget limit for a particular category. Some popular budgeting apps include Mint, PocketGuard, and YNAB.

If you prefer to track your expenses manually, you can use a spreadsheet or a notebook. Write down every expense, no matter how small. Be sure to include everything from rent and utilities to groceries and entertainment. Once you have a few months' worth of data, you can start to analyze your spending patterns and make adjustments.

When tracking your expenses, it is essential to be honest with yourself. Don't try to hide or justify unnecessary purchases. Instead, be realistic about your spending habits and look for areas where you can cut back. For example, if you notice that you are spending too much money on eating out, try cooking at home more often.

Another way to track your expenses is to use cash instead of credit or debit cards. When you use cash, you are more aware of your spending, and it can be easier to stick to your budget. You can also use the envelope system, where you allocate a certain amount of cash for each category and put it in an envelope. When the money in the envelope is gone, you know you have reached your budget limit for that category.

Tracking expenses is a vital tool for reducing debt and achieving financial stability. Whether you use a budgeting app, a spreadsheet, or cash, the key is to be honest with yourself and make adjustments where necessary. With a little bit of effort and discipline, you can take control of your finances and build a better future for yourself and your family.

Making Adjustments to the Budget
Creating a budget is an essential step in reducing debt, but sometimes unexpected expenses can throw off even the most carefully crafted plan. When this happens, it's important to adjust the budget accordingly.

Here are some tips for making adjustments to your budget:

1. Prioritize necessary expenses: If unexpected expenses arise, prioritize the necessary ones. This includes things like housing, food, and transportation. These expenses should always take priority over discretionary spending.

2. Review your budget: Take a look at your current budget and see where you can make adjustments. Are there any areas where you can cut back? Maybe you can reduce your cable bill, or cut back on dining out. Every little bit helps.

3. Increase your income: If you find that you're consistently struggling to make ends meet, you may need to increase your income. Consider taking on a part-time job or freelance work. You can also look into government assistance programs that can help supplement your income.

4. Use credit wisely: If you must use credit to cover unexpected expenses, be sure to use it wisely. Only charge what you can afford to pay back in full at the end of the month. Avoid using high-interest credit cards, and consider getting a low-interest personal loan instead.

5. Revisit your budget regularly: Your budget should be a living document that changes with your financial situation. Revisit it regularly to make sure it's still working for you. If you find that it's not, make the necessary adjustments. Remember, making adjustments to your budget is a normal part of the process. Don't beat yourself up if unexpected expenses throw off your plan. Just adjust and keep moving forward. With dedication and perseverance, you can reduce your debt and achieve financial freedom.

Chapter 3: Saving Strategies

The importance of saving cannot be overstated, especially for those living on a tight budget or struggling with debt. Saving money can help you build a safety net for unforeseen emergencies, reduce debt, and improve your overall financial health.

For low-income families, saving may seem like an impossible task. However, even small amounts saved regularly can add up over time. It's important to prioritize saving in your budget, even if it means cutting back on other expenses. One way to make saving easier is to automate your savings. Set up a direct deposit to a savings account each paycheck, and you won't even have to think about it. Another option is to save any unexpected windfalls, such as tax refunds or bonuses, instead of spending them.

Saving also allows you to take advantage of compound interest. By leaving your savings in an interest-bearing account, your money will grow over time. This can help you reach your financial goals faster, whether it's paying off debt or saving for a down payment on a home. For parents, saving is even more important. Not only does it provide a safety net for emergencies, but it also allows you to invest in your child's future. Starting a college fund or saving for extracurricular activities can ensure that your child has the opportunities they need to succeed. In addition to saving, it's important to budget wisely. By tracking your expenses and prioritizing your spending, you can reduce debt and build your savings at the same time.

Look for ways to cut back on unnecessary expenses, such as eating out or subscription services.

Saving is a vital component of reducing debt and improving your financial health. Even small amounts saved regularly can make a big difference over time. Prioritizing saving in your budget and automating your savings can make it easier to reach your financial goals, whether it's paying off debt or investing in your child's future.

Saving on a tight budget
Saving on a tight budget is a crucial aspect of debt reduction and financial stability.
It can be challenging, especially for those who are living on a low income or struggling to make ends meet. However, with the right mindset and strategies, anyone can start saving money and improving their financial situation.

The first step to saving on a tight budget is to track your spending. You need to know where your money is going and identify areas where you can cut back. This can be done by keeping a spending journal or using a budgeting app. Once you have a clear picture of your spending habits, you can start making adjustments.

One of the most effective ways to save money is by reducing your expenses. This can be achieved by cutting back on non-essential items such as eating out, entertainment, and clothing. Instead, focus on necessities like food, housing, and transportation. Consider buying generic brands, using coupons, and shopping during sales to save money on groceries.

Another strategy for saving on a tight budget is to create a savings plan. This involves setting a specific goal and allocating a portion of your income towards saving each month. You can start small, with just a few dollars a week, and gradually increase the amount as you become more comfortable with saving.

If you have children, it can be challenging to save money on a tight budget. However, there are several strategies that can help.

Consider buying second-hand clothes and toys, preparing meals at home, and using public transportation instead of owning a car.

You can also involve your children in the saving process by teaching them about money management and encouraging them to save their allowance.

By tracking your spending, reducing your expenses, creating a savings plan, and involving your children in the process, you can start building a solid financial foundation and reducing your debt. Remember, every penny counts, and small changes can make a big difference in the long run.Strategies for saving money on groceries, bills, and other expenses
One of the biggest challenges that low-income families face is stretching their monthly budget to meet their everyday needs. Groceries, bills, and other expenses can quickly pile up, leaving little room for savings or unexpected expenses. However, with the right strategies, it's possible to cut costs and save money without sacrificing quality of life.

One of the best ways to save money on groceries is to plan your meals ahead of time. This not only helps you avoid impulse purchases but also allows you to take advantage of sales and bulk discounts.

Make a list of the ingredients you need for each meal and stick to it when you go shopping. Try to buy in-season produce and generic brands, which are often cheaper than name-brand products.

Another way to save money on groceries is to buy in bulk. Consider purchasing non-perishable items like rice, pasta, and canned goods in larger quantities, which often come at a lower price per unit. You can also save money by buying meat in bulk and freezing it for later use. When it comes to bills, there are several strategies you can use to reduce your monthly expenses. One of the best is to negotiate with your service providers. Call your internet, cable, and phone providers and ask if they can offer you a better deal or discount.

You may be surprised at how much money you can save by simply asking.

Another way to save money on bills is to cut back on unnecessary services. Do you really need that premium cable package or unlimited data plan? Consider downgrading to a more affordable plan that meets your basic needs. Finally, be mindful of your other expenses, such as entertainment and dining out.

Instead of going to expensive restaurants or buying pricey movie tickets, look for free or low-cost activities in your area.

You can also save money by cooking at home instead of eating out.

There are many strategies for saving money on groceries, bills, and other expenses. By planning ahead, buying in bulk, negotiating with service providers, and cutting back on unnecessary expenses, you can reduce your debt and live a more financially stable life.

Ways to Increase Income

When you're living on a tight budget, it can be challenging to find ways to increase your income. However, there are several options available that can help you boost your income and improve your financial situation.

Here are some ideas to consider:

1. Look for a side hustle

A side hustle is a great way to earn extra income outside of your regular job.

There are many options available, such as freelance writing, dog walking, or driving for a ride-sharing service like Uber or Lyft.

Consider your skills and interests and look for opportunities that align with them.

2. Sell unwanted items

If you have items that you no longer need or use, consider selling them to earn extra cash. You can sell items online through websites like eBay, Craigslist, or Facebook Marketplace. You can also have a yard sale or sell items to a consignment shop.

3. Participate in paid surveys

Many companies offer paid surveys to consumers to gather feedback on their products or services. You can sign up for these surveys online and earn money for sharing your opinions.

4. Rent out a room

If you have a spare room in your home, consider renting it out on websites like Airbnb or HomeAway. This can be a great way to earn extra income and meet new people.

5. Look for part-time work

If you have the time and availability, consider looking for part-time work to supplement your income. This can be anything from working at a retail store to delivering pizzas.

6. Start a small business

If you have a particular skill or talent, consider starting a small business. You can offer services like lawn care, house cleaning, or tutoring. This can be a great way to earn extra income on your own terms.

Increasing your income can help you pay off debt faster and improve your overall financial situation.

Chapter 4: Debt Reduction Techniques

Debt is an inevitable part of life. Most people at some point in their lives will have to borrow money or take out a loan to finance a major purchase such as a home or car.

However, debt can quickly spiral out of control and become a burden that is difficult to escape. For low-income families, debt can be even more crippling, leading to financial instability and poverty.

Understanding debt is the first step towards reducing it. Debt is essentially money that you owe to someone else. This could be a credit card company, a bank, or even a friend or family member. When you borrow money, you agree to pay it back with interest over a certain period of time. The interest is the cost of borrowing the money and is usually expressed as a percentage of the total amount borrowed.

The problem with debt is that it can quickly grow out of control if you don't manage it properly. If you miss payments or only make the minimum payment each month, the interest will continue to accrue, and your debt will continue to grow. This can lead to a cycle of debt that is difficult to escape.

The good news is that there are ways to reduce debt, even on a tight budget.

The first step is to create a budget and stick to it. This means tracking your income and expenses and finding ways to cut back on unnecessary spending. You can also look for ways to increase your income by taking on a side hustle or selling items you no longer need.

Another option for low-income families is to seek out debt relief programs. These programs can help you negotiate with creditors to reduce your debt or create a repayment plan that is more manageable. Some programs even offer financial education and counseling to help you avoid future debt problems.

Ultimately, the key to reducing debt is to take control of your finances and make a plan to pay off your debts. This may require sacrifices and lifestyle changes, but the long-term benefits are worth it. With determination and a little bit of penny pinching, you can reduce your debt and achieve financial stability.

Prioritizing Debt Payments

If you're struggling with debt on a tight budget, it can feel overwhelming to know where to start. But the first step is to prioritize your debt payments. This means deciding which debts to focus on paying off first, based on their interest rates and other factors.

Here are some tips for prioritizing your debt payments:

1. Start with high-interest debts. If you have credit card debt or payday loans with high interest rates, these should be your top priority. These types of loans can quickly spiral out of control if you don't pay them off quickly, so make them your first focus.

2. Consider secured debts. If you have a car loan or a mortgage, these are secured debts, meaning that the lender can repossess the car or foreclose on the house if you don't make your payments. While you don't want to fall behind on any debt payments, make sure you prioritize these secured debts so you don't risk losing your assets.

3. Look at the minimum payments. While you want to focus on paying off high-interest debts first, make sure you're still making the minimum payments on all your debts. Falling behind on payments can hurt your credit score and make it harder to get out of debt in the long run.

4. Consider debt consolidation or refinancing. If you have multiple debts with high interest rates, it may be worth looking into debt consolidation or refinancing options.

These can help you lower your interest rates and simplify your payments.

5. Don't forget about other bills. While paying off debt should be a priority, you still need to pay your other bills, like rent, utilities, and groceries. Make sure you're budgeting for these expenses as well.

By prioritizing your debt payments, you can start chipping away at your debt and making progress towards financial freedom.

Remember, it's not going to happen overnight, but with a little persistence and dedication, you can reduce your debt and improve your financial situation.

Strategies for Paying off Debt

If you are struggling with debt, you are not alone. Many low-income families are living paycheck to paycheck and find it challenging to make ends meet. The good news is that there are strategies you can use to pay off your debt and reduce your financial stress.

1. Create a Budget

The first step in paying off your debt is to create a budget. A budget will help you identify your income and expenses and give you a clear picture of your financial situation. Once you have a budget, you can start making changes to reduce your expenses and increase your income.

2. Cut Expenses

Cutting expenses is an essential part of paying off debt. Look for ways to reduce your monthly bills, such as canceling subscriptions or negotiating lower rates on your utilities. You can also save money by buying generic brands, cooking at home, and shopping for deals.

3. Increase Income

Increasing your income is another way to pay off debt. You can start by looking for ways to make extra money, such as taking on a part-time job or selling items you no longer need. You can also ask for a raise at work or look for a higher-paying job.

4. Prioritize Debt

When you have multiple debts, it's essential to prioritize which ones to pay off first.

One strategy is to pay off the debt with the highest interest rate first. This will save you money on interest in the long run. Another strategy is to pay off the smallest debt first, which can give you a sense of accomplishment and motivation to continue paying off your debts.

5. Consolidate Debt

If you have multiple debts with high-interest rates, consolidating your debt into one loan with a lower interest rate can help you save money and pay off your debt faster.

You can also consider transferring your credit card balances to a card with a lower interest rate.

Paying off debt requires discipline, commitment, and patience. By creating a budget, cutting expenses, increasing income, prioritizing debt, and consolidating debt, you can reduce your debt and improve your financial situation. Remember, every little bit counts, and even small changes can make a big difference in the long run.

Negotiating with creditors
Negotiating with creditors can be a daunting task, but it is an essential step towards reducing your debt. It involves communicating with your creditors to find a mutually agreeable solution that will help you pay off your debt while keeping your finances in order.
It is a crucial step towards achieving financial stability, especially for those who are struggling financially.

If you are a low-income family, negotiating with creditors can help you reduce your debt and avoid bankruptcy. Here are some tips to help you negotiate with your creditors:

1. Understand your financial situation: Before you start negotiating with your creditors, it is essential to understand your financial situation. You need to know how much debt you owe, your income, and your expenses.

This information will help you determine how much you can afford to pay your creditors each month.

2. Contact your creditors: Once you have a clear understanding of your financial situation, contact your creditors to discuss your debt. Explain your financial situation and propose a payment plan that you can afford. Be honest and straightforward about your financial situation, and be prepared to negotiate.

3. Be persistent: Negotiating with creditors can take time, and it may require several attempts to reach an agreement. Be persistent and keep trying until you find a solution that works for you.

4. Seek professional help: If you are struggling to negotiate with your creditors, seek professional help. A debt counselor or financial advisor can help you negotiate with your creditors and find a solution that works for you.

Negotiating with creditors is an essential step towards reducing your debt, especially if you are a low-income family. It requires persistence, honesty, and a clear understanding of your financial situation. If you are struggling to negotiate with your creditors, seek professional help to find a solution that works for you. Remember, negotiating with creditors is a crucial step towards achieving financial stability, and it is never too late to start.

Chapter 5: Debt Relief Programs for Low-Income Families

If you are struggling with debt and finding it difficult to keep up with payments, there are government programs available that can provide debt relief. These programs are designed to help low-income families and individuals who are facing financial hardship. One such program is the Debt Management Plan (DMP), which is offered by credit counseling agencies. A DMP allows you to consolidate your debts into one monthly payment and negotiate with your creditors to reduce interest rates and fees.

This can help you pay off your debt faster and with less stress.

Another program that can provide debt relief is the Debt Settlement Program (DSP). This program involves negotiating with your creditors to settle your debts for less than what you owe. While this may sound too good to be true, it is important to understand that this program can have a negative impact on your credit score and may not be suitable for everyone.

For those struggling with student loan debt, there are government programs available such as Income-Driven Repayment (IDR) plans. These plans allow you to make payments based on your income, which can make it easier to manage your monthly expenses.

Additionally, low-income families may be eligible for government assistance programs such as Temporary Assistance for Needy Families (TANF) and Supplemental Nutrition Assistance Program (SNAP). These programs provide financial assistance for basic needs such as food, housing, and medical care.

It is important to note that while government programs can provide debt relief, they are not a quick fix and require commitment and dedication to overcome debt. It is also important to research and understand the terms and conditions of each program before enrolling.

If you are struggling with debt, there are government programs available that can provide debt relief. These programs are designed to help low-income families and individuals who are facing financial hardship.

It is important to research and understand the terms and conditions of each program before enrolling to ensure that it is the best option for your situation.

Non-profit organizations that offer debt relief services
Debt can be a significant burden for low-income families, making it difficult to make ends meet and achieve financial stability. Fortunately, there are non-profit organizations that offer debt relief services to help families reduce and manage their debt.

Here are some of the most reputable ones:

1. National Foundation for Credit Counseling (NFCC)

NFCC is a non-profit organization that has been helping people with debt management for over 60 years. They offer free credit counseling services, debt management plans, and financial education programs to help individuals and families get out of debt and stay debt-free. NFCC has over 600 member agencies across the country, making it easy for people to access their services.

2. Consumer Credit Counseling Service (CCCS)

CCCS is another non-profit organization that offers free credit counseling services and debt management plans.

They work with creditors to negotiate lower interest rates and payments and help people pay off their debts faster. CCCS also provides budgeting and financial education to help people improve their money management skills.

3. Debt Reduction Services (DRS)

DRS is a non-profit organization that specializes in debt settlement and debt management services. They work with creditors to negotiate lower payments and settlements and help people pay off their debt in a reasonable amount of time.

DRS also provides financial education and budgeting advice to help people avoid getting into debt again in the future.

4. United Way

United Way is a non-profit organization that provides a range of services to help low-income families, including debt relief services. They offer financial education programs, credit counseling, and debt management plans to help people get out of debt and stay debt-free. United Way also provides other services, such as food assistance, housing, and healthcare, to help families meet their basic needs.

If you are struggling with debt and need help, these non-profit organizations can provide you with the support and guidance you need to get back on track. Don't hesitate to reach out to them for assistance. With their help, you can reduce your debt and achieve financial stability.Tips for working with debt relief professionals

Debt relief professionals can provide valuable assistance to individuals who are struggling with debt. However, it is essential to approach the process with caution and diligence to avoid falling prey to scams or ineffective practices. Here are some tips for working with debt relief professionals:

1. Do your research

Before hiring a debt relief professional, it is crucial to conduct thorough research.

Check their credentials and qualifications, read reviews and testimonials from previous clients, and verify their legitimacy with relevant authorities.

2. Understand the terms and fees

Be sure to understand the terms and fees associated with the debt relief program.

Ask for a breakdown of all costs and fees, and ensure that they are reasonable and transparent. Avoid working with professionals who make unrealistic promises or charge exorbitant fees.

3. Communicate effectively

Clear communication is key when working with debt relief professionals.

Be honest and transparent about your financial situation, and ask questions when you do not understand something. Keep in touch with the professional throughout the process to ensure that everything is on track.

4. Follow through on commitments

Debt relief professionals can only help you if you are committed to the process.

Be sure to follow through on all commitments, such as making payments on time and providing necessary documentation.

Failure to do so can jeopardize the success of the program.

5. Keep a record

Document all communication and transactions with the debt relief professional. This will help you track progress and ensure that everything is being handled appropriately. If you encounter any issues, having a record can also be useful in resolving disputes. Working with debt relief professionals can be a valuable tool in reducing debt on a tight budget. However, it is essential to approach the process with caution and diligence to ensure that you are working with a reputable professional who can provide effective assistance.

Chapter 6: The Psychology of Money

Debt can be a heavy burden that affects not only your finances but also your emotional well-being. It can cause stress, anxiety, and depression, affecting your relationships, work, and overall quality of life.

Understanding the emotional impact of debt is crucial when trying to overcome it and improve your financial situation.

One of the main emotional effects of debt is stress. When you owe money, you may constantly worry about how to pay it back, how much interest you're accumulating, and how it's affecting your credit score. This stress can lead to physical symptoms like headaches, insomnia, and even heart problems.

Another emotional impact of debt is shame and guilt. You may feel like you made bad decisions that led you into debt, or that you're not capable of managing your finances.

This shame can make it difficult to seek help or talk to others about your situation.

Debt can also cause anxiety about the future. You may worry about how you'll pay for unexpected expenses, how you'll save for retirement, or how you'll provide for your family. This anxiety can make it difficult to enjoy the present and plan for the future.

Understanding the emotional impact of debt is the first step towards overcoming it.

It's important to acknowledge your feelings and seek support from family, friends, or a financial counselor. You can also try stress-reducing activities like exercise, meditation, or spending time in nature.

Reducing your debt through budgeting and saving can also help alleviate the emotional impact of debt. When you have a plan in place, you'll feel more in control of your finances and less stressed about your future.

Start by tracking your expenses, creating a budget, and finding ways to save money. Small changes like cutting back on unnecessary expenses, cooking at home, and using coupons can add up over time.

Debt relief programs for low-income families can also help reduce the emotional impact of debt. These programs can provide assistance with debt negotiation, debt consolidation, and debt settlement. They can also offer financial education and counseling to help you manage your finances more effectively.

Debt can have a significant emotional impact on your life. It's important to understand these effects and seek support to overcome them. By reducing your debt through budgeting and saving, and seeking help from debt relief programs, you can take control of your finances and improve your overall well-being.

Strategies for Changing Money Mindset

Changing your money mindset is a crucial step towards achieving financial stability and reducing debt on a tight budget.

Here are some strategies that can help you change your money mindset:

1. Focus on the big picture

One of the most important strategies for changing your money mindset is to focus on the big picture. This means setting long-term financial goals and working towards them. Start by creating a budget, tracking your expenses, and identifying areas where you can cut back. Then, set a goal to pay off your debts and save for emergencies and retirement.

2. Practice gratitude

Gratitude is a powerful tool that can help you change your money mindset. Instead of focusing on what you don't have, focus on what you do have. Take some time each day to reflect on the things you're grateful for, whether it's your health, your family, or your job. This can help you shift your focus from scarcity to abundance.

3. Develop a growth mindset

A growth mindset is the belief that you can learn and grow, even in difficult circumstances. This can be especially helpful when it comes to managing money. Instead of feeling stuck in your current financial situation, focus on what you can do to improve it. Learn new skills, seek out opportunities for growth, and be open to feedback.

4. Avoid comparison

One of the biggest traps when it comes to money mindset is comparison. It's easy to look at others who seem to have more than you and feel like you're not doing enough. However, this can lead to feelings of inadequacy and a scarcity mindset. Instead, focus on your own progress and celebrate your successes, no matter how small they may seem.

5. Surround yourself with positive influences

Finally, surround yourself with positive influences. This can mean finding a financial mentor, joining a support group, or simply spending time with people who have a positive attitude towards money. By surrounding yourself with people who encourage and support you, you'll be more likely to stay motivated and on track towards your financial goals.

Changing your money mindset is an essential step towards reducing debt on a tight budget. By focusing on the big picture, practicing gratitude, developing a growth mindset, avoiding comparison, and surrounding yourself with positive influences, you can transform your relationship with money and achieve financial stability.

Developing Healthy Spending Habits
Developing healthy spending habits is crucial if you want to reduce debt and achieve financial stability. It is important to understand that your spending habits are the key to your financial success. Without healthy spending habits, you will continue to struggle with debt, no matter how much money you earn.

Here are some tips to help you develop healthy spending habits:

1. Create a budget

Creating a budget is the first step in developing healthy spending habits. A budget is a plan that helps you understand how much money you have coming in and going out. It allows you to allocate your money in a way that aligns with your financial goals.

2. Track your spending

Tracking your spending is essential to developing healthy spending habits. It helps you identify areas where you may be overspending and allows you to make adjustments to your budget accordingly.

3. Cut unnecessary expenses

Cutting unnecessary expenses is a critical step in developing healthy spending habits. It involves identifying expenses that you can live without and eliminating them from your budget. This may include eating out less, canceling subscription services, or reducing your cable bill.

4. Save for emergencies

Saving for emergencies is an essential part of developing healthy spending habits. Emergencies can happen at any time, and having a savings buffer can help you avoid going further into debt.

5. Avoid impulse purchases

Avoiding impulse purchases is another critical aspect of developing healthy spending habits. Impulse purchases are purchases that you make on a whim without considering whether you can afford them or not. These purchases can quickly add up and lead to debt.

Developing healthy spending habits takes time and effort, but it is worth it in the end. By following these tips, you can reduce your debt, achieve financial stability, and improve your overall quality of life. Remember, small changes can make a big difference, so start today!

Chapter 7: Long-Term Financial Planning

Creating long-term financial goals is crucial for anyone, regardless of their income level.

It's especially important for those who are struggling financially to have a clear understanding of their financial situation and where they want to be in the future.

By setting long-term financial goals, you can create a roadmap for your financial future and take steps to achieve your dreams.

The first step in creating long-term financial goals is to define what you want to achieve. Do you want to be debt-free? Do you want to save for a down payment on a house? Do you want to retire early? Whatever your goals may be, it's important to be as specific as possible. This will help you stay focused and motivated as you work towards achieving them.

Once you have defined your goals, it's time to create a plan to achieve them.

This plan should include specific actions that you will take to reach your goals. For example, if your goal is to pay off your credit card debt, your plan may include creating a budget, cutting back on expenses, and increasing your income through a side hustle.

It's important to remember that achieving long-term financial goals takes time and patience. It may take months or even years to reach your goals, but with dedication and hard work, it is possible. It's also important to review your goals regularly and make adjustments as needed. Life may throw unexpected curveballs, and your goals may need to be modified to reflect these changes.

Creating long-term financial goals is an essential step towards achieving financial stability and success. By defining your goals and creating a plan to achieve them, you can take control of your finances and build a brighter future for yourself and your family. Remember, it's never too late to start setting and working towards your financial goals.

Building Wealth Through Investments
Investments are a great way to build wealth, especially if you are trying to reduce your debt on a tight budget. While it may seem daunting, investing can be done by anyone, regardless of your income level. In this chapter, we will discuss how to build wealth through investments.

1. Start Small

When it comes to investing, starting small is the key. It doesn't matter how much you have to invest, what matters is that you start. You can start by investing in stocks, bonds, mutual funds, or even real estate. The key is to start with a small amount and gradually increase your investment as your income grows.

2. Diversify Your Investments

Diversifying your investments is crucial if you want to build wealth. This means investing in different types of assets such as stocks, bonds, and real estate. By diversifying your investments, you reduce your risk and increase your chances of making a profit.

3. Invest in Index Funds

Index funds are a great way to invest in the stock market without having to pick individual stocks. Index funds are a type of mutual fund that tracks a specific market index, such as the S&P 500. By investing in index funds, you can get exposure to a broad range of stocks and reduce your risk.

4. Take Advantage of Tax-Advantaged Accounts

Tax-advantaged accounts such as 401(k)s and IRAs can help you build wealth by reducing your taxes and increasing your savings. These accounts allow you to contribute pre-tax dollars, which means you don't have to pay taxes on the money until you withdraw it.

5. Reinvest Your Dividends

If you invest in stocks that pay dividends, reinvesting those dividends can help you build wealth over time. When you reinvest your dividends, you buy more shares of the stock, which means you will receive more dividends in the future.

Planning for Retirement

Retirement may seem like a far-off dream for many poor people, but it is never too early to start planning for your golden years. With careful budgeting and saving, even those with limited incomes can build a nest egg that will provide financial security and peace of mind in retirement.

The first step in planning for retirement is to set realistic goals. Calculate how much money you will need to live comfortably in retirement, taking into account factors such as inflation, healthcare costs, and any outstanding debts. This will give you a clear idea of how much you need to save each month to reach your retirement goals.

Next, explore your retirement savings options. If your employer offers a 401(k) plan or other retirement benefits, take advantage of these programs. Many employers also offer matching contributions, which means that for every dollar you contribute, your employer will match it up to a certain amount. This is essentially free money that can help you reach your retirement goals faster.

If you are self-employed or your employer does not offer retirement benefits, consider opening an Individual Retirement Account (IRA). There are two types of IRA accounts: traditional and Roth. Traditional IRAs allow you to deduct contributions from your taxable income, while Roth IRAs do not. Both types of accounts have their own advantages and disadvantages, so it is important to research which option is best for your specific financial situation.

In addition to retirement savings accounts, you can also build your retirement nest egg through other savings strategies. For example, consider investing in stocks or mutual funds that have a history of strong returns. Real estate can also be a good long-term investment, provided you do your research and invest wisely.

Finally, remember that planning for retirement is an ongoing process. Review your retirement goals regularly and adjust your savings strategies as needed. With dedication and hard work, even those with limited incomes can achieve financial security in retirement.

Chapter 8: Conclusion

In this book, we have explored the power of penny pinching and how it can help you reduce debt on a tight budget. We understand that as a low-income family, debt can be a significant burden on your finances, but with the right strategies and mindset, you can overcome it. Here are some key takeaways from our discussion:

1. Budgeting is crucial: The first step to reducing debt is creating a budget. You need to know exactly where your money is going, and where you can cut back on expenses. You can use budgeting apps or spreadsheets to help you keep track of your income and expenses.

2. Cut back on unnecessary expenses: Once you have a budget in place, look for any expenses that you can cut back on. This may include eating out less, canceling subscription services, or finding cheaper alternatives for everyday items.

3. Save, save, save: Saving is an essential part of debt reduction. Even if you can only save a small amount each month, it will add up over time. Consider setting up automatic savings transfers to make the process easier.

4. Use debt repayment strategies: There are several debt repayment strategies you can use, such as the debt snowball or debt avalanche method. Figure out which one works best for you and stick to it.

5. Seek professional help: If you are struggling to manage your debt, seek professional help. Nonprofit organizations such as credit counseling agencies can provide you with guidance and support.

As parents, it is essential to teach your children about the importance of budgeting and saving. Teach them early on about the value of money and how to manage it effectively.

Reducing debt on a tight budget is possible. It requires discipline, patience, and a willingness to make sacrifices. By implementing the strategies outlined in this book, you can take control of your finances and start building a brighter financial future for yourself and your family.

Encouragement to Continue Penny Pinching and Reducing Debt

It's easy to lose motivation when it comes to penny pinching and reducing debt, especially when it seems like the progress is slow or non-existent. However, it's important to remember that every little bit counts and to stay committed to the journey. Here are some reasons why it's important to continue penny pinching and reducing debt, and some tips on how to stay motivated.

Firstly, reducing debt can improve your financial standing and increase your credit score. A good credit score is essential for getting approved for loans, mortgages, and even rental applications. Additionally, reducing debt can lead to less stress and more financial freedom. It can also help you avoid high-interest payments that can accumulate over time and cause more debt.

Secondly, penny pinching can help you save money for emergencies and unexpected expenses. It's important to have a safety net for unexpected situations like car repairs, medical bills, or job loss. Saving even a small amount each month can add up over time and make a big difference when you need it the most.

To stay motivated, it's important to set achievable goals and celebrate small victories along the way. For example, setting a goal to pay off a certain amount of debt each month or saving a certain amount each paycheck can give you a sense of accomplishment and keep you motivated. Celebrating these victories, no matter how small, can help you stay positive and focused on your goal.

Another way to stay motivated is to find support from friends, family, or online communities. There are many resources available for debt reduction and penny pinching, and connecting with others who are on the same journey can provide motivation and accountability.

Penny pinching and reducing debt can be a challenging journey, but it's important to stay committed and motivated. Remember the benefits of reducing debt and saving money, celebrate small victories, and find support from others. With perseverance and determination, you can achieve financial freedom and peace of mind.

Final Thoughts on the Power of Penny Pinching

In today's world, where the cost of living is skyrocketing, it is becoming increasingly difficult for low-income families to make ends meet. Most of these families find themselves struggling with overwhelming debt, and it seems like an impossible task to get out of the vicious cycle of debt. The good news is that penny pinching is a powerful tool that can help you reduce your debt and regain control of your finances.

Through this book, we have discussed various penny pinching techniques that can help you save money and reduce your debt.

From creating a budget to cutting down on unnecessary expenses, we have covered a range of strategies that can help you achieve your financial goals. We hope that by implementing these techniques, you will be able to reduce your debt and take control of your financial future.

One of the key takeaways from this book is the importance of having a budget. A budget helps you track your income and expenses, and it allows you to identify areas where you can cut back. By creating a budget and sticking to it, you can avoid overspending and save money that can be used to pay off your debt.

Another important aspect of penny pinching is cutting down on unnecessary expenses.

This can include things like eating out less, reducing your utility bills, and avoiding impulse purchases. By being mindful of your spending habits, you can save money and put it towards paying off your debt.

In conclusion, penny pinching is a powerful tool that can help you reduce your debt and achieve financial freedom. It is not an easy task, and it requires discipline and dedication. However, by implementing the strategies outlined in this book, you can take control of your finances and work towards a debt-free future. We hope that this book has been helpful, and we wish you all the best in your journey towards financial stability.

About the author

Benjamin Warson is a renowned author specializing in personal finance and debt reduction. He is widely recognized for his practical strategies and insights in helping individuals overcome financial challenges.

His book, "The Power of Penny Pinching: How to Reduce Debt on a Tight Budget," has received acclaim for its accessible approach and relatable examples.

Warson is also a sought-after speaker at financial conferences, where he inspires audiences with his empowering presentations on debt management and financial planning. Through his expertise and dedication, Warson has made a significant impact on individuals striving for financial stability and independence.

www.ingramcontent.com/pod-product-compliance
Lightning Source LLC
Chambersburg PA
CBHW070118230526

45472CB00004B/1311